CRYPTO CLARITY:

DEMYSTIFYING BITCOIN AND BLOCKCHAIN FOR BEGINNERS

ROBERT C. KNIGHT

CONTENTS

INTRODUCTION

Welcome to **Crypto Clarity: Demystifying Bitcoin and Blockchain for Beginners**. In the rapidly evolving landscape of finance and technology, cryptocurrencies and blockchain technology have emerged as transformative forces. They have captured the imagination of individuals, businesses, and even governments, promising new ways to think about money, security, and trust in the digital age.

For those taking their first steps into this exciting and dynamic realm, the world of cryptocurrency and blockchain can seem daunting, filled with technical jargon, complex concepts, and rapidly changing developments. This is where Crypto Clarity: Demystifying Bitcoin and Blockchain for Beginners comes in – as your trusted guide to navigate the intricate landscape of cryptocurrencies and blockchain technology.

Unlocking the Mysteries

This book is designed for beginners – individuals who are curious, eager to learn, and ready to embark on a journey of discovery. Whether you've heard about Bitcoin and blockchain in passing conversations, seen headlines in the news, or simply want to understand the technology reshaping our financial future, you're in the right place.

Crypto Clarity: Demystifying Bitcoin and Blockchain for Beginners is your key to unlock the mysteries surrounding Bitcoin and blockchain. We recognize that the world of cryptocurrency can be complex, but we believe that with the right guidance and explanations, anyone can grasp the fundamental concepts and principles that underpin this digital revolution.

What You'll Find Inside

In the chapters ahead, we will unravel the core concepts of cryptocurrency and blockchain technology step by step. We'll start with the basics, providing clear explanations and real-world examples to demystify complex ideas. You'll gain a solid understanding of what Bitcoin is, how it works, and why it matters. We'll delve into blockchain technology, exploring its applications beyond cryptocurrency and its potential to transform various industries.

We'll also address practical aspects, guiding you on how to buy, store, and use cryptocurrencies safely and responsibly. You'll learn about the diverse world of cryptocurrencies, including altcoins and tokens, and discover how to navigate the landscape of exchanges and wallets.

Beyond the technical aspects, we'll explore the broader implications of cryptocurrencies and blockchain technology. You'll gain insights into the evolving regulatory landscape, the impact on traditional finance, and the innovative projects and trends shaping the future of the digital economy.

Your Empowerment Matters

Understanding the principles and mechanisms behind cryptocurrencies and blockchain technology empowers you to make informed decisions, whether you're considering an investment, exploring career opportunities, or simply staying informed about the evolving digital landscape.

We aim to provide you with a comprehensive, yet accessible resource that demystifies the complex world of cryptocurrency and blockchain. As you progress through this book, we encourage you to ask questions, seek clarity, and engage with the material. Our goal is to equip you with the knowledge and confidence needed to navigate this exciting frontier.

Your Journey Begins Now

So, are you ready to embark on this enlightening journey? This guide is here to accompany you every step of the way, ensuring that the world of Bitcoin and blockchain is not only understandable but also filled with possibilities waiting to be explored.

Let's start unraveling the mysteries and charting a course through the world of cryptocurrency and blockchain technology. Your adventure begins now.

CHAPTER 1: INTRODUCTION TO CRYPTOCURRENCY

Understanding the Basics

Cryptocurrency has emerged as a game-changer in the world of finance and technology. For many, it represents a revolutionary shift in how we think about money, transactions, and trust. In this chapter, we will delve deep into the fundamentals of cryptocurrency, uncovering the essential concepts that underpin this transformative technology.

What is Cryptocurrency?

At its core, cryptocurrency is a type of digital or virtual currency that uses cryptographic techniques for security. Unlike traditional currencies issued and regulated by governments (fiat currencies like the US Dollar or Euro), cryptocurrencies are decentralized and operate on blockchain technology. Let's break down some key components:

1. Decentralization:

Decentralization is a foundational concept in the world of cryptocurrencies. Unlike fiat currencies controlled by central banks or governments, cryptocurrencies operate on decentralized networks of computers. These networks are maintained and secured by a distributed community of users, often referred to as nodes. Decentralization means that no single entity has full control over the currency, making it resistant to manipulation, censorship, and single points of failure.

2. Blockchain Technology:

Blockchain is the technology that powers the majority of cryptocurrencies. It can be thought of as a public ledger, recording all transactions across a network of computers. Each group of transactions is bundled into a "block," and these blocks are linked together in a chronological order to form a "chain" of blocks - hence, the term "blockchain." Once data is added to a block, it becomes nearly impossible to alter, ensuring the security and immutability of the information.

3. Cryptography:

The term "cryptocurrency" itself highlights the importance of cryptography in this field. Cryptography is used to secure transactions, control the creation of new units of cryptocurrency, and verify the transfer of assets. Each participant in a cryptocurrency network has a pair of cryptographic keys: a public key and a private key. The public key is used to generate an address, which is visible to others on the blockchain. The private key, on the other hand, is kept secret and is used to sign transactions, proving ownership. This cryptographic infrastructure provides a high level of security and ensures the integrity of the system.

4. Digital Ownership:

When you own cryptocurrencies, what you really have is control over a private key associated with a specific address on the blockchain. This private key is your digital signature, allowing you to access and manage your digital assets. It's crucial to safeguard your private key because if it's lost or compromised, you risk losing control of your cryptocurrencies. Unlike traditional physical assets, cryptocurrencies exist solely in digital form, and ownership is determined by these cryptographic keys.

5. Transactions:

At its core, the primary purpose of cryptocurrency is to facilitate digital transactions. These transactions involve the transfer of digital assets (cryptocurrencies) from one user's digital wallet to another's. When a transaction is initiated, it's verified by the network and recorded on the blockchain. This transparent and secure process eliminates the need for intermediaries, such as banks, and ensures the authenticity of each transaction. Cryptocurrency transactions are typically faster than traditional financial systems, and they can occur 24/7, without regard for banking hours or international borders.

The Evolution of Money

Understanding the historical context of money is essential to appreciate the significance of cryptocurrencies in today's financial landscape. The concept of money has undergone a remarkable transformation throughout human history, reflecting the evolving needs and complexities of human society.

1. Barter System:

In the earliest human societies, people engaged in direct barter, exchanging goods and services with each other. While this system worked to some extent, it had significant limitations. For a barter trade to occur, both parties had to have something the other wanted. This requirement for a double coincidence of wants made barter cumbersome and inefficient, especially as societies grew more complex.

2. Commodity Money:

To overcome the limitations of barter, societies transitioned to using commodity money. Commodity money consisted of items with intrinsic value, such as grains, cattle, or precious metals like gold and silver. These commodities were widely accepted in trade because of their inherent worth. This form of money helped facilitate trade and represented a significant advancement in the evolution of money.

3. Fiat Currency:

As economies expanded and became more sophisticated, governments and central authorities introduced fiat currency. Unlike commodity money, fiat money has no intrinsic value. Instead, its value is derived from the trust and authority of the government that issues it. Most of the world's currencies today, including the US Dollar and the Euro, are fiat currencies. Fiat currencies offer flexibility and ease of use, but they are also susceptible to inflation and government control.

4. Digital Money:

With the rise of the internet, traditional fiat currencies transitioned into digital forms. Digital money allowed for online transactions, electronic banking, and the digitization of financial services. This shift provided significant convenience for consumers and businesses, reducing the reliance on physical cash.

5. Cryptocurrency:

The introduction of Bitcoin in 2009 by the pseudonymous Satoshi Nakamoto marked a significant milestone in the history of money. Bitcoin is a decentralized digital currency that operates independently of any central authority. It was designed to address many of the limitations of traditional currencies and banking systems. Bitcoin's creation was prompted by the global financial crisis of 2008 and a desire to create a trustless, transparent, and censorship-resistant form of money.

Cryptocurrencies like Bitcoin rely on cryptographic principles and blockchain technology to provide security, transparency, and decentralization. They enable peer-to-peer transactions without the need for intermediaries, reducing fees and increasing financial inclusivity. This innovative approach to money has led to the proliferation of thousands of cryptocurrencies, each with its unique features and use cases.

The historical journey from barter systems to cryptocurrencies illustrates how societies have continually sought more efficient, secure, and accessible forms of money. Cryptocurrencies, with their decentralized nature and technological advancements, represent the next evolutionary step in this millennia-long process.

The Promise of Cryptocurrency

As you embark on your journey to understand cryptocurrencies, it's essential to recognize the promise they hold. Cryptocurrencies offer several key advantages:

1. Decentralization and Security:

The decentralized nature of cryptocurrencies makes them highly secure. Transactions are recorded on a distributed ledger, making it extremely challenging for malicious actors to manipulate the system. Security breaches, such as hacking or fraud, are far less common than in traditional banking.

2. Transparency:

Blockchain technology provides transparency by recording all transactions on a public ledger. This transparency reduces the potential for corruption and fraud, as anyone can audit the blockchain to verify transactions.

3. Reduced Fees:

Traditional financial systems often involve intermediaries, each of which charges fees for their services. Cryptocurrency transactions, especially those within the same network, typically have lower fees because they eliminate the need for intermediaries.

4. Financial Inclusion:

Cryptocurrencies have the potential to bring financial services to the unbanked and underbanked populations worldwide. With internet access and a digital wallet, individuals in remote or underserved areas can participate in the global economy.

5. Borderless Transactions:

Cryptocurrencies are not tied to specific countries or regions, making them ideal for cross-border transactions. They can simplify international trade and remittances by reducing the complexity and cost of currency exchange.

6. Ownership and Control:

Cryptocurrency holders have direct ownership and control over their digital assets. This is in contrast to traditional banks, where individuals may have limited control over their accounts and assets.

7. Innovation and Use Cases:

Cryptocurrencies have spurred innovation in various industries, from finance to supply chain management. Smart contracts, decentralized finance (DeFi) platforms, and non-fungible tokens (NFTs) are just a few examples of the novel applications of blockchain technology.

In the following chapters of this book, we will explore these advantages in more detail and provide practical guidance on how to navigate the world of cryptocurrency. Whether you are interested in using cryptocurrency for everyday transactions, investing, or understanding its potential impact on the global economy, this book will equip you with the knowledge and tools needed to navigate this exciting and dynamic field.

In conclusion, the introduction to cryptocurrency and the evolution of money sets the stage for a deeper exploration of this transformative technology. It's a journey that promises to challenge conventional notions of currency and finance, offering new possibilities and opportunities for individuals and businesses alike. With a solid understanding of the basics, you're well-prepared to embark on this exciting adventure into the world of cryptocurrency.

CHAPTER 2: THE BIRTH OF BITCOIN

Who is Satoshi Nakamoto?

The story of Bitcoin begins with an enigmatic figure known as Satoshi Nakamoto. The identity of Satoshi Nakamoto remains one of the most significant mysteries in the world of cryptocurrency and technology. To this day, nobody knows for sure who Satoshi is, whether it's an individual or a group of people, or even if they are still alive. Satoshi Nakamoto's creation of Bitcoin in 2008 marked the beginning of the cryptocurrency revolution.

The Pseudonym

Satoshi Nakamoto is a pseudonym, and the individual or group behind it has taken great care to conceal their true identity. The name itself is of Japanese origin, and it's believed to be a combination of two common Japanese names: "Satoshi" and "Nakamoto." However, this pseudonym has never been definitively linked to a real-world identity.

The choice of a pseudonym is an intriguing aspect of Bitcoin's early history. Satoshi's decision to use a pseudonym might have been driven by a desire to remain anonymous, protect their privacy, or avoid potential legal or regulatory scrutiny. It's important to note that pseudonyms are not uncommon in the world of open-source software development, where contributors often use online monikers.

The Whitepaper

The first public glimpse of Satoshi Nakamoto's vision came in October 2008 when a person or group using the name Satoshi Nakamoto published the Bitcoin whitepaper titled "Bitcoin: A Peer-to-Peer Electronic Cash System." This whitepaper outlined the principles and mechanics of Bitcoin, introducing the concept of a decentralized digital currency based on blockchain technology.

In the whitepaper, Nakamoto outlined the challenges faced by traditional financial systems, such as the reliance on intermediaries like banks and the potential for double-spending (spending the same money more than once). Nakamoto proposed a novel solution: a decentralized network of computers that would validate and record transactions on a public ledger, ensuring transparency and security. This system would become the basis for Bitcoin.

The release of the whitepaper was a watershed moment. It not only presented a groundbreaking idea but also provided a practical blueprint for its implementation. Satoshi Nakamoto's ability to combine technical expertise with clear communication laid the foundation for the Bitcoin network's development and growth.

Contributions and Disappearances

Satoshi Nakamoto actively participated in the development of Bitcoin in its early days. They communicated with a growing community of developers and enthusiasts through online forums and email. Nakamoto's guidance and coding expertise were instrumental in the initial stages of Bitcoin's development.

However, as Bitcoin gained popularity and its community grew, Satoshi Nakamoto gradually faded from the public eye. In December 2010, Nakamoto made their last known public communication, expressing concerns about the increasing centralization of Bitcoin development. They handed over control of the Bitcoin source code repository to a group of developers and subsequently vanished from the public space.

This departure only deepened the mystery surrounding Nakamoto's identity. Speculations and investigations into Nakamoto's identity have continued for years, but no conclusive evidence has emerged. Some have suggested that Nakamoto's disappearance was a deliberate act to allow Bitcoin to thrive without a central figurehead, emphasizing the cryptocurrency's decentralized nature.

The Mystery Continues

Numerous theories and investigations have been conducted to uncover the true identity of Satoshi Nakamoto. Journalists, researchers, and curious enthusiasts have attempted to piece together clues from Nakamoto's writings, online activities, and contributions to the Bitcoin codebase. However, despite these efforts, the identity of Satoshi remains undisclosed.

One theory suggests that Nakamoto is a collective effort of multiple individuals rather than a single person. This theory is based on the depth and breadth of knowledge demonstrated in Nakamoto's writings and code contributions. It's argued that it would be challenging for a single person to possess such expertise in cryptography, economics, and software development.

While the mystery of Satoshi Nakamoto's identity remains unsolved, the lasting legacy of their creation, Bitcoin, continues to shape the world of finance and technology. Bitcoin's development has been carried forward by a vibrant and dedicated community of developers, miners, investors, and enthusiasts who believe in the vision laid out in Nakamoto's whitepaper.

How Bitcoin Works

Understanding how Bitcoin works is essential for anyone interested in delving into the world of cryptocurrencies. At its core, Bitcoin is a decentralized digital currency that operates on a peer-to-peer network. Here's a detailed look at how the technology behind Bitcoin functions:

Blockchain Technology

Blockchain is the foundation of Bitcoin. It's a distributed ledger that records all transactions across the Bitcoin network. The blockchain consists of a chain of blocks, each containing a group of transactions. New blocks are added to the chain approximately every ten minutes through a process called **mining**.

Mining

Mining is the process by which new Bitcoin transactions are validated and added to the blockchain. Miners use powerful computers to solve complex mathematical puzzles, and the first miner to solve the puzzle gets the privilege of adding a new block to the blockchain. In return, they are rewarded with a certain number of newly created Bitcoins and transaction fees.

Mining serves multiple purposes in the Bitcoin network:

- **Transaction Verification:** Miners ensure the validity of new transactions by confirming that the sender has the required balance and the transaction has not been double-spent.

- **Security:** The computational work required for mining provides security to the network, making it difficult for malicious actors to alter the blockchain's history.
- **Issuing New Bitcoins:** Mining is the mechanism through which new Bitcoins are created and introduced into circulation. This process is known as the "block reward."

Over time, the difficulty of the mathematical puzzles increases to ensure that new blocks are added roughly every ten minutes. This process, known as "difficulty adjustment," maintains the predictable issuance rate of new Bitcoins.

Transactions

Bitcoin transactions involve the transfer of digital assets (Bitcoins) from one user to another. Each transaction is represented as a digital signature, which is a cryptographic proof that the transaction is valid. Once a transaction is broadcast to the network, it is verified by nodes (computers) on the network.

Wallets and Addresses

To use Bitcoin, individuals need a **Bitcoin wallet**. A wallet is a software program that allows users to send, receive, and store their Bitcoins securely. Each wallet has one or more **Bitcoin addresses**, which are essentially like account numbers. Addresses are derived from the user's public key, and they are used to receive Bitcoins.

Public and Private Keys

Behind each Bitcoin address are two cryptographic keys: a **public key** and a **private key**. The public key is shared openly and serves as an address for receiving Bitcoin. However, the private key must remain secret and is used to sign transactions, proving ownership of the Bitcoins associated with a particular address.

Here's how the process works:

- **Alice wants to send Bitcoins to Bob.**
- **Alice uses her private key to create a digital signature for the transaction.**
- **The transaction, along with the digital signature, is broadcast to the network.**
- **Nodes on the network verify the digital signature using Alice's public key to ensure that the transaction is legitimate.**
- **Once verified, the transaction is added to the pool of unconfirmed transactions.**
- **Miners select transactions from the pool and include them in a new block.**
- **The block is mined, and the transaction is confirmed.**

This cryptographic process ensures the security and integrity of Bitcoin transactions while preserving the privacy and ownership of users.

Decentralization and Security

One of Bitcoin's core strengths is its decentralization. Unlike traditional financial systems, there is no central authority controlling Bitcoin. Transactions are verified by nodes on the network, and the blockchain provides transparency and security by recording all transactions in an immutable ledger.

Decentralization makes Bitcoin resistant to censorship, manipulation, and single points of failure. It empowers individuals to have full control over their finances without the need for intermediaries.

Limited Supply

Bitcoin has a limited supply of 21 million coins. This scarcity is programmed into the Bitcoin protocol and is achieved through a process called **halving**. Approximately every four years, the number of new Bitcoins generated through mining is halved. This scarcity is often compared to precious metals like gold and is seen as a key factor in Bitcoin's store of value.

Peer-to-Peer Transactions

Bitcoin enables peer-to-peer transactions, meaning users can send and receive money directly without relying on intermediaries like banks. This eliminates the need for third-party trust and reduces transaction fees.

Anonymity vs. Transparency

While Bitcoin transactions are pseudonymous, meaning they are not directly tied to real-world identities, the blockchain is entirely transparent. Anyone can view the transaction history of any Bitcoin address on the blockchain. This transparency is one of the reasons Bitcoin is often described as "pseudonymous" rather than fully anonymous.

Scalability and Challenges

Bitcoin's success has led to challenges related to scalability. As the network has grown, it has faced congestion and higher fees during periods of increased activity. To address these issues, various scaling solutions have been proposed and implemented, such as the Lightning Network, which allows for faster and cheaper transactions by conducting some transactions off-chain.

The Impact and Future of Bitcoin

Understanding the birth and mechanics of Bitcoin is crucial for anyone looking to explore the world of cryptocurrencies further. Bitcoin's creation by Satoshi Nakamoto represented a groundbreaking solution to long-standing problems in traditional finance. Its potential to disrupt financial systems, empower individuals, and serve as a store of value has garnered worldwide attention.

In the following chapters, we will delve into more practical aspects of using and investing in Bitcoin, as well as explore the broader implications of this innovative technology. We will also discuss the evolving regulatory landscape surrounding cryptocurrencies and their role in the global economy.

In conclusion, Satoshi Nakamoto's creation of Bitcoin and the subsequent development of the Bitcoin network have reshaped the way we think about money, trust, and financial systems. As you continue your journey into the world of cryptocurrency, you'll discover the many opportunities and challenges that come with this transformative technology.

CHAPTER 3: THE BLOCKCHAIN REVOLUTION

Exploring Distributed Ledger Technology

The blockchain revolution represents a fundamental shift in the way we think about trust, data management, and transparency. At its heart lies a groundbreaking technology known as **distributed ledger technology (DLT)**, with blockchain being the most well-known and widely used form of DLT. In this chapter, we will explore the core concepts of DLT and how it has the potential to reshape industries far beyond cryptocurrencies.

Understanding Distributed Ledger Technology

Distributed Ledger Technology is a concept that challenges the traditional centralized approach to data management. Unlike centralized systems, where data is stored and controlled by a single entity or authority, DLT operates on a decentralized network of computers. This network, or ledger, is maintained by a distributed community of users, often referred to as nodes.

Key features of DLT include:

1. **Decentralization:** DLT networks have no central point of control. Instead, data is stored across multiple nodes, making it highly resistant to manipulation or single points of failure.
2. **Immutability:** Once data is recorded on the ledger, it is extremely difficult to alter. This immutability is achieved through cryptographic techniques and consensus mechanisms.
3. **Transparency:** DLTs provide transparency by making data accessible to all participants in the network. Transactions and data entries are visible and auditable.
4. **Security:** The decentralized nature of DLTs enhances security by reducing the vulnerability to hacks and cyberattacks. Data is protected through encryption and consensus mechanisms.

How Distributed Ledgers Work

At the core of a distributed ledger is a database that records transactions or data entries. These entries are grouped into blocks, which are linked together in chronological order, forming a chain of blocks – the blockchain. Let's break down the process:

1. **Transaction Creation:** Participants in the network initiate transactions. These transactions can represent financial transfers, digital asset exchanges, or any form of data entry.
2. **Verification:** Transactions are verified by network nodes through a consensus mechanism. In the case of Bitcoin and many other cryptocurrencies, this consensus mechanism is known as proof-of-work (PoW).

Other DLTs use alternative mechanisms like proof-of-stake (PoS) or delegated proof-of-stake (DPoS). The consensus mechanism ensures that only valid transactions are added to the ledger.

3. **Adding to the Ledger:** Once verified, the transactions are grouped into a block. The block is then added to the blockchain through a process known as mining (in PoW systems). In PoS and DPoS systems, blocks are created and added by validators or delegates.
4. **Immutability:** Once a block is added to the blockchain, it is nearly impossible to alter any of the transactions within it. This immutability is a critical feature that ensures the integrity of the data.

Beyond Cryptocurrency: Use Cases of DLT

While cryptocurrencies were the first and remain one of the most prominent use cases for DLT, the technology's potential extends far beyond digital currencies. Here are some notable applications:

1. Supply Chain Management:

DLT can be used to track the movement of goods throughout the supply chain. This increases transparency, reduces fraud, and enables more efficient recalls in cases of product defects.

2. Smart Contracts:

Smart contracts are self-executing contracts with the terms of the agreement directly written into code. DLT allows for the creation and execution of smart contracts, automating processes such as payments, asset transfers, and more.

3. Voting Systems:

DLT can enhance the security and transparency of voting systems. It can prevent tampering with election results and ensure that votes are accurately counted.

4. Healthcare Records:

Healthcare providers can use DLT to securely and efficiently manage patient records. Patients can have control over their data, granting access to specific healthcare providers as needed.

5. Cross-Border Payments:

DLT can streamline cross-border payments, reducing the time and cost associated with international transactions. This has the potential to revolutionize the financial industry.

6. Real Estate:

DLT can simplify property transactions by reducing paperwork and ensuring the accuracy of ownership records. This could lead to more efficient and transparent real estate markets.

Challenges and Considerations

While DLT holds immense promise, it is not without its challenges and considerations:

1. Scalability:

Blockchain networks, in particular, face scalability issues. As more transactions are added to the blockchain, the network can become slower and less efficient. Solutions like sharding and layer-2 scaling are being explored to address this challenge.

2. Energy Consumption:

Proof-of-work blockchains, like Bitcoin, are criticized for their high energy consumption. This has led to discussions around the environmental impact of blockchain technology.

3. Regulatory Concerns:

Governments and regulatory bodies are still grappling with how to classify and regulate cryptocurrencies and DLT. Legal frameworks are evolving, and compliance can vary significantly by jurisdiction.

4. Interoperability:

Different blockchain networks often operate in isolation. Achieving interoperability – the ability of different networks to communicate and interact with each other – is a complex challenge that requires standardization efforts.

5. Privacy:

While DLT provides transparency, some applications require privacy. Ensuring privacy while maintaining transparency is a delicate balance that needs to be addressed in DLT design.

Security and Transparency

One of the most compelling aspects of distributed ledger technology, particularly blockchain, is the combination of **security** and **transparency**. These two attributes are at the heart of what makes DLT a revolutionary technology with the potential to transform industries.

Security

DLT enhances security in several ways:

1. **Decentralization:** Unlike centralized systems that have single points of failure, DLT operates on a network of distributed nodes. This means that no single entity has control over the entire system, reducing the risk of attacks or manipulation.
2. **Cryptography:** DLT relies on advanced cryptographic techniques to secure transactions and data. Each transaction is digitally signed and cannot be altered once added to the blockchain. Public and private keys protect access to wallets and ensure that only authorized parties can initiate transactions.
3. **Consensus Mechanisms:** Consensus mechanisms like proof-of-work (PoW) and proof-of-stake (PoS) require network participants to reach an agreement on the validity of transactions. This consensus process adds a layer of security, as malicious actors would need to control a significant portion of the network's computing power or tokens to compromise the system.
4. **Immutability:** Once data is recorded on the blockchain, it is extremely difficult to change. This immutability ensures that historical records remain intact and trustworthy.
5. **Audibility:** The transparent nature of DLT allows for easy auditing of transactions. Anyone can inspect the blockchain to verify transactions, making it a powerful tool against fraud and corruption.

Transparency

DLT provides transparency through the following mechanisms:

1. **Public Ledger:** In many DLT systems, including public blockchains, the ledger is publicly accessible. This means that anyone can view the entire transaction history, promoting openness and accountability.
2. **Real-Time Updates:** Transactions are added to the blockchain in near real-time. This provides real-time visibility into data, enabling faster decision-making and reducing the need for intermediaries.
3. **Auditable Records:** The immutable nature of DLT ensures that once a transaction is recorded, it cannot be altered. This creates a permanent and auditable record of all activities on the network.
4. **Trustless Transactions:** DLT allows participants to engage in transactions without the need for trust in a central authority. Instead, trust is established through cryptographic proofs and consensus mechanisms.

The Balance between Security and Transparency

DLT strikes a delicate balance between security and transparency. While it provides a high level of security through encryption, decentralization, and consensus, it also ensures transparency by making data accessible to all participants.

This balance is particularly valuable in industries where trust is crucial but intermediaries introduce inefficiencies and vulnerabilities. For example, in financial services, blockchain technology can reduce the risk of fraud while providing transparency into transactions. In supply chain management, it can ensure the authenticity and origin of products while maintaining a clear record of their journey.

However, it's important to recognize that not all DLT systems are created equal. The level of security and transparency can vary based on the design and governance of the network.

Different DLT platforms may prioritize one attribute over the other, depending on their intended use case.

Conclusion

As we conclude our exploration of distributed ledger technology in the context of the blockchain revolution, we've witnessed the profound impact it can have on trust, security, and transparency. DLT's decentralized nature, supported by cryptography and consensus mechanisms, offers new possibilities for industries ranging from finance to healthcare, and from supply chain management to voting systems.

In the chapters that follow, we will continue our journey into the world of cryptocurrencies and blockchain, delving deeper into practical applications, investment strategies, and the evolving regulatory landscape. Armed with a solid understanding of DLT, you're well-prepared to explore the exciting opportunities and challenges that lie ahead in this transformative technology.

CHAPTER 4: WALLETS AND ADDRESSES

Storing and Managing Your Cryptocurrency

In the world of cryptocurrencies, owning digital assets like Bitcoin, Ethereum, or Litecoin is akin to having a digital wallet full of digital coins and tokens. However, unlike physical wallets that you can hold in your hand, these digital wallets exist solely in the digital realm. They serve as your gateway to the world of cryptocurrencies, allowing you to send, receive, and store your digital wealth securely. In this chapter, we will explore the essential components of cryptocurrency wallets and addresses, empowering you to manage your digital assets with confidence.

What Is a Cryptocurrency Wallet?

A **cryptocurrency wallet** is a software program or a hardware device that enables users to store, manage, and interact with their cryptocurrencies. These wallets play a crucial role in the cryptocurrency ecosystem, serving as the interface between users and the blockchain networks that power digital currencies. Here are some key points to understand about cryptocurrency wallets:

1. **Digital Storage:** Cryptocurrency wallets store the cryptographic keys necessary to access and manage your digital assets. These keys are not physical objects but rather complex strings of characters that grant ownership and control of your cryptocurrencies.
2. **Security:** The security of your wallet is paramount. Losing access to your wallet's keys can mean losing access to your digital assets permanently. Therefore, it's crucial to choose a secure wallet and take appropriate security measures.
3. **Functionality:** Wallets come in various forms, each with its own set of features and functions. Some wallets are designed for simplicity and ease of use, while others offer advanced features for power users.

Types of Cryptocurrency Wallets

Cryptocurrency wallets can be categorized into several types, each with its own advantages and considerations. Here are the primary types of cryptocurrency wallets:

1. Software Wallets:

- **Online Wallets:** These wallets operate on web-based platforms and are accessible through a web browser. They are convenient but can be vulnerable to online attacks.
- **Mobile Wallets:** Mobile wallets are designed for smartphones and provide a user-friendly and portable way to manage your cryptocurrencies.
- **Desktop Wallets:** Desktop wallets are installed on your computer and offer more security than online wallets. They give you full control over your private keys.

2. Hardware Wallets:

- **Hardware wallets** are physical devices specifically designed for securely storing cryptocurrencies. They are considered one of the most secure options as they are offline (not connected to the internet) and immune to online threats.

3. Paper Wallets:

- A **paper wallet** involves printing your cryptocurrency's public and private keys on a physical piece of paper. It is a form of "cold storage" and is highly secure as it is offline. However, it requires careful handling to prevent physical damage or loss.

4. Brain Wallets:

- A **brain wallet** relies on memorization. You generate a private key based on a passphrase or a series of words that you commit to memory. While it offers security from physical theft, it is vulnerable to forgotten passphrases or dictionary attacks.

Public and Private Keys

To understand cryptocurrency wallets fully, you must grasp the concepts of **public keys** and **private keys**. These cryptographic keys are at the core of wallet security and functionality.

Public Key:

A **public key** is a long string of characters that serves as your cryptocurrency wallet's receiving address. It's a bit like your bank account number. You can freely share your public key with anyone to receive cryptocurrencies. When someone sends you digital assets, they use your public key to specify the destination.

Private Key:

A **private key**, on the other hand, is a secret, alphanumeric string that is mathematically linked to your public key. Think of it as the password or key to your digital wallet. It is crucial to keep your private key confidential, as anyone with access to it can control the cryptocurrencies associated with your wallet. Losing your private key means losing access to your digital assets.

Here's how the process works:

1. **Generating the Keys:** When you create a new cryptocurrency wallet, a pair of keys is generated – a public key (receiving address) and a private key (the secret to accessing your funds).

2. **Sending Cryptocurrency:** When someone wants to send you cryptocurrency, they use your public key (receiving address) to specify the destination of the funds.

3. **Accessing Your Cryptocurrency:** To access and manage the cryptocurrencies sent to your wallet, you use your private key. This private key is used to sign transactions, proving ownership of the digital assets.

4. **Security Considerations:** It is absolutely crucial to keep your private key secure. Never share it with anyone, and consider storing it offline or on a secure hardware wallet.

The Importance of Backups

Losing access to your private key means losing access to your digital assets. This is why creating backups of your keys is of utmost importance. Here are some backup strategies to consider:

1. **Paper Backup:** For software wallets, consider creating a paper backup of your private key or seed phrase (a series of words that can be used to regenerate your private key). Store this paper backup in a secure and physically safe location.
2. **Hardware Wallet Backup:** Hardware wallets often provide a recovery seed phrase that allows you to restore your wallet in case the device is lost or damaged. Write down this seed phrase and store it securely.
3. **Multiple Backups:** Consider creating multiple backups and storing them in different secure locations. This provides redundancy and mitigates the risk of losing access to your funds due to a single point of failure.

Security Best Practices

As the saying goes, "With great power comes great responsibility." The power to manage your digital assets also means the responsibility to safeguard them. Here are some security best practices for managing your cryptocurrency wallet:

1. **Use Strong Passwords:** If your wallet requires a password, choose a strong, unique, and complex passphrase that is difficult for others to guess.
2. **Enable Two-Factor Authentication (2FA):** If your wallet or exchange offers 2FA, enable it. This adds an additional layer of security by requiring a one-time code from your mobile device to access your wallet.

3. **Beware of Phishing:** Be cautious of phishing attempts. Verify the authenticity of websites and emails, and never enter your private key or seed phrase on suspicious sites.
4. **Keep Software Updated:** Ensure that your wallet software and operating system are up-to-date with the latest security patches.
5. **Regular Backups:** Regularly backup your private keys or seed phrases and store them securely.
6. **Secure Your Devices:** Protect the devices you use for cryptocurrency transactions with strong passwords, encryption, and security software.
7. **Offline Storage:** Consider using hardware wallets or offline storage methods for long-term storage of significant amounts of cryptocurrency.
8. **Educate Yourself:** Continuously educate yourself about cryptocurrency security best practices and stay informed about potential threats.

Conclusion

Cryptocurrency wallets and addresses are your gateway to the world of digital wealth. Understanding the importance of securing your private keys, choosing the right type of wallet, and implementing robust security practices is crucial to safeguard your assets in the ever-evolving landscape of cryptocurrencies. In the following chapters, we will delve further into practical aspects of using cryptocurrencies, exploring the diverse world of digital assets, and discussing strategies for responsible investment and storage. Armed with this knowledge, you'll be well-prepared to navigate the exciting world of cryptocurrencies with confidence.

CHAPTER 5: BUYING YOUR FIRST BITCOIN

Choosing the Right Exchange

Before you can become a proud owner of Bitcoin, you'll need to choose a cryptocurrency exchange – an online platform that facilitates the buying, selling, and trading of cryptocurrencies. The exchange you select will play a critical role in your cryptocurrency journey, impacting your user experience, security, fees, and the range of cryptocurrencies available to you. In this chapter, we will guide you through the process of choosing the right exchange to make your first Bitcoin purchase a smooth and secure experience.

What Is a Cryptocurrency Exchange?

A **cryptocurrency exchange** is an online marketplace where individuals can buy, sell, trade, or exchange cryptocurrencies. These platforms act as intermediaries that facilitate cryptocurrency transactions, much like traditional stock exchanges facilitate the trading of stocks and securities.

Key characteristics of cryptocurrency exchanges include:

1. **Access to Multiple Cryptocurrencies:** Exchanges typically offer a variety of cryptocurrencies beyond

Bitcoin, including Ethereum, Litecoin, Ripple, and many others. This allows you to diversify your crypto portfolio.

2. **User-Friendly Interfaces:** Most exchanges strive to provide user-friendly interfaces and tools to make it easy for users to navigate the platform, place orders, and manage their accounts.
3. **Security Measures:** Reputable exchanges prioritize security, employing various measures such as two-factor authentication (2FA), cold storage of funds, and regular security audits to protect user assets.
4. **Liquidity:** Liquidity refers to how easily an asset can be bought or sold without affecting its price significantly. Larger, well-established exchanges typically have higher liquidity, allowing for smoother trading experiences.
5. **Fiat Currency Support:** Some exchanges allow you to buy cryptocurrencies with traditional fiat currencies like the US dollar, euro, or yen. This simplifies the process for newcomers.

Types of Cryptocurrency Exchanges

Cryptocurrency exchanges come in various types, each catering to different user needs and preferences:

1. Centralized Exchanges (CEXs):

- **Features:** Centralized exchanges are operated by a centralized organization. They offer a wide range of cryptocurrencies, trading pairs, and user-friendly interfaces.

- **Security:** Security measures vary, but reputable CEXs invest heavily in security protocols. However, they may be vulnerable to hacking.
- **User Base:** Centralized exchanges tend to have larger user bases and higher liquidity.
- **Examples:** Coinbase, Binance, Kraken, Bitstamp.

2. Decentralized Exchanges (DEXs):

- **Features:** Decentralized exchanges operate without a central authority. They allow users to trade directly from their wallets, providing greater control and privacy.
- **Security:** DEXs are considered more secure against hacks since they do not store user funds. However, they may have lower liquidity.
- **User Base:** DEXs are gaining popularity but typically have smaller user bases compared to CEXs.
- **Examples:** Uniswap, SushiSwap, PancakeSwap.

3. Peer-to-Peer Exchanges (P2P):

- **Features:** Peer-to-peer exchanges connect buyers and sellers directly, allowing them to negotiate terms and conduct transactions without intermediaries.
- **Security:** Security depends on user conduct and the platform's reputation. Escrow services are often used to mitigate risks.
- **User Base:** P2P exchanges cater to users looking for privacy and direct transactions. User bases can vary widely.
- **Examples:** LocalBitcoins, Paxful, Bisq.

Factors to Consider When Choosing an Exchange

Selecting the right exchange for your first Bitcoin purchase is crucial. Consider the following factors to make an informed decision:

1. *Security:*

- Research the exchange's security practices, including how they store and protect user funds. Look for platforms with a history of strong security measures and a transparent approach to security.

2. *User Experience:*

- Evaluate the exchange's user interface and overall user experience. A user-friendly platform can make your first Bitcoin purchase more accessible and enjoyable.

3. *Fees:*

- Be aware of the fees associated with the exchange. These may include trading fees, withdrawal fees, deposit fees, and others. Compare fee structures across different platforms.

4. *Liquidity:*

- Consider the liquidity of the exchange, especially if you plan to trade frequently. Higher liquidity typically results in tighter bid-ask spreads, reducing trading costs.

5. *Supported Cryptocurrencies:*

- Check if the exchange offers the cryptocurrencies you are interested in, not just Bitcoin. Some exchanges specialize in altcoins, while others focus primarily on Bitcoin and a few major cryptocurrencies.

6. Geographical Availability:

- Ensure the exchange is available in your region. Some exchanges have geographical restrictions, and access may vary based on your location.

7. Regulatory Compliance:

- Confirm that the exchange complies with relevant regulations in your country. Regulatory compliance can impact the safety and legality of your transactions.

8. Customer Support:

- Explore the level of customer support provided by the exchange. Responsive customer support can be invaluable in case you encounter issues.

9. Reviews and Reputation:

- Read reviews and gather feedback from other users. Look for exchanges with a positive reputation and a history of satisfied customers.

10. Privacy Considerations:

- Consider your privacy preferences. Some exchanges require extensive identity verification, while others offer more privacy-focused options.

11. Payment Methods:

- Check the available payment methods on the exchange. Ensure it supports the method you intend to use, whether it's bank transfers, credit cards, or other options.

Making Your First Purchase

Once you've selected a suitable exchange, it's time to take the step and make your first Bitcoin purchase. Here's a step-by-step guide:

Step 1: Create an Account

- Sign up for an account on the chosen exchange. You'll need to provide personal information and complete identity verification in compliance with Know Your Customer (KYC) regulations.

Step 2: Secure Your Account

- Enable two-factor authentication (2FA) for an added layer of security. This typically involves receiving a one-time code on your mobile device each time you log in.

Step 3: Deposit Funds

- Deposit funds into your exchange account. Depending on the exchange, you can fund your account using bank transfers, credit/debit cards, or other payment methods.

Step 4: Place an Order

- Navigate to the trading section of the exchange. Specify the amount of Bitcoin you want to buy and the price at which you are willing to buy it. You can choose between different order types, such as market orders or limit orders.

Step 5: Confirm and Execute

- Review your order details, including the fees associated with the transaction. Once you are satisfied, confirm the order, and the exchange will execute it.

Step 6: Securely Store Your Bitcoin

- After the purchase is complete, transfer your Bitcoin to a secure cryptocurrency wallet. Avoid leaving your digital assets on the exchange, as they can be vulnerable to hacking.

Step 7: Keep Records

- Maintain records of your transactions, including purchase details, dates, and any associated fees. These records can be helpful for tax reporting and tracking your investment.

Step 8: Stay Informed

- Continue to educate yourself about cryptocurrency markets, trends, and security best practices. Staying informed will help you make informed decisions as you navigate the world of digital assets.

Conclusion

Buying your first Bitcoin is a significant step into the world of cryptocurrencies. By choosing the right exchange and following best practices for security and transaction management, you can embark on your cryptocurrency journey with confidence. Remember that the cryptocurrency landscape is continually evolving, so staying informed and adapting to changes will be essential as you explore this exciting and transformative digital frontier.

CHAPTER 6:
BEYOND BITCOIN:
ALTCOINS AND TOKENS

Exploring the Crypto Ecosystem

While Bitcoin holds the distinction of being the pioneer and most well-known cryptocurrency, the world of digital assets extends far beyond the boundaries of the original cryptocurrency. These alternative digital currencies, often referred to as **altcoins**, have emerged with unique features, use cases, and technologies, each seeking to address specific challenges or offer innovative solutions. In this chapter, we will explore the diverse and ever-evolving crypto ecosystem, introducing you to altcoins and tokens, and providing insights into their significance in the broader landscape of cryptocurrencies.

What Are Altcoins?

The term **altcoin** is a portmanteau of "alternative" and "coin," and it refers to any cryptocurrency other than Bitcoin. Altcoins are created with the intention of improving or altering aspects of the original Bitcoin protocol, whether that be its underlying technology, security, or features. The world of altcoins is vast and continually expanding, encompassing a wide range of projects and use cases. Let's delve into some of the key characteristics and categories of altcoins:

1. Technological Variations:

- Many altcoins introduce technical innovations to the original Bitcoin blockchain. These innovations can include faster transaction times, enhanced security features, and different consensus algorithms.

2. Use Cases:

- Altcoins are often designed to cater to specific use cases beyond peer-to-peer digital currency. Examples include smart contract platforms, privacy coins, and tokens for decentralized applications (dApps).

3. Market Capitalization:

- Altcoins vary in market capitalization, with some having smaller market values and others rivaling or surpassing Bitcoin in terms of capitalization. Ethereum, for instance, is one of the most well-known altcoins and boasts a substantial market cap.

4. Decentralization:

- The degree of decentralization can differ among altcoins. Some may replicate Bitcoin's decentralized model, while others may have more centralized governance structures.

5. Competing with Bitcoin:

- Some altcoins aim to compete directly with Bitcoin as a digital currency. They offer different features and benefits to attract users, such as faster confirmation times or improved scalability.

6. ICO Boom:

- The Initial Coin Offering (ICO) boom of the late 2010s led to the creation of numerous altcoins. These projects raised funds by offering their own tokens to the public in exchange for established cryptocurrencies like Bitcoin or Ethereum.

Prominent Altcoins

Several altcoins have gained significant popularity and recognition in the cryptocurrency space. Here are a few prominent examples:

1. Ethereum (ETH):

- Ethereum is a decentralized platform that enables the creation of smart contracts and decentralized applications (dApps). It introduced the concept of the Ethereum Virtual Machine (EVM), allowing developers to build and deploy smart contracts.

2. Ripple (XRP):

- Ripple aims to enable fast and low-cost cross-border payments. It operates on a unique consensus algorithm known as the Ripple Protocol Consensus Algorithm (RPCA).

3. Litecoin (LTC):

- Often referred to as the "silver to Bitcoin's gold," Litecoin is a peer-to-peer cryptocurrency designed for fast and low-cost transactions.

4. Cardano (ADA):

- Cardano is a blockchain platform known for its focus on sustainability, scalability, and interoperability. It uses a unique consensus algorithm called Ouroboros.

5. Chainlink (LINK):

- Chainlink is a decentralized oracle network that connects smart contracts with real-world data and external systems.

6. Polkadot (DOT):

- Polkadot is a multi-chain network that enables different blockchains to interoperate, enhancing scalability and flexibility.

These are just a few examples, and the altcoin landscape is incredibly diverse, with new projects and innovations constantly emerging. The significance of altcoins lies in their ability to provide users with choices and address specific needs or challenges within the broader cryptocurrency ecosystem.

Understanding Utility Tokens

As you explore the world of cryptocurrencies, you'll come across another significant category of digital assets: **utility tokens**. Unlike Bitcoin and many altcoins, utility tokens are not primarily intended to serve as a digital currency or store of value. Instead, they have specific functions and use cases within blockchain-based ecosystems, applications, or platforms.

Here are key aspects to understand about utility tokens:

1. Utility Within a Specific Ecosystem:

- Utility tokens are often designed to represent ownership or access rights within a particular blockchain network or decentralized application. They are not meant for general transactions but rather to perform specific functions.

2. Incentivizing Use:

- Utility tokens can incentivize users to engage with and participate in a blockchain ecosystem. They may be required to access certain features, execute smart contracts, or contribute to network security.

3. Not Necessarily Tradable:

- While utility tokens can be bought and sold on cryptocurrency exchanges, their primary purpose is to be used within the associated ecosystem. They are not primarily intended for speculative trading.

4. Examples of Use:

- Utility tokens can serve various purposes. For example, within the Ethereum ecosystem, Ether (ETH) is considered both a cryptocurrency and a utility token used for paying transaction fees and executing smart contracts. In contrast, Basic Attention Token (BAT) is used in the Brave browser ecosystem to reward content creators and users for their attention.

5. Initial Coin Offerings (ICOs):

- Utility tokens are often distributed through ICOs, where project developers sell tokens to raise capital for their blockchain-based projects.

6. Regulatory Considerations:

- The regulatory status of utility tokens can vary by jurisdiction. In some cases, they may be classified as securities, while in others, they may be considered digital commodities or assets.

7. Examples of Utility Tokens:

- Tether (USDT): Used for price stability and as a medium of exchange on various blockchain platforms.
- Binance Coin (BNB): Used within the Binance exchange ecosystem for trading fee discounts and various services.
- Chainlink (LINK): Used to pay node operators and access real-world data in the Chainlink network.

The Role of Utility Tokens in Decentralized Applications (dApps)

One of the most common applications of utility tokens is within decentralized applications (dApps). These dApps are built on blockchain platforms, and utility tokens are used to facilitate various functions and interactions within these applications.

Here are some examples of how utility tokens can be utilized in dApps:

1. **Decentralized Finance (DeFi):** In the DeFi ecosystem, utility tokens are used for lending, borrowing, yield farming, and liquidity provision within decentralized platforms.
2. **Gaming and Virtual Worlds:** Utility tokens are used to represent in-game assets, enable virtual item trad-

ing, and incentivize player engagement in blockchain-based games.

3. **Content Creation:** In platforms like Steem or Hive, users are rewarded with utility tokens for creating and curating content. These tokens can then be traded, staked, or converted into other cryptocurrencies.
4. **Supply Chain and Logistics:** Utility tokens can be employed to track and verify the authenticity and provenance of physical goods throughout the supply chain, enhancing transparency and traceability.
5. **Predictive Markets:** In prediction markets, users can create and participate in markets using utility tokens to forecast events and outcomes.
6. **Decentralized Identity and Authentication:** Utility tokens can be used to verify and authenticate identity within decentralized identity platforms.

Challenges and Considerations

While utility tokens have the potential to enable innovative and decentralized applications, they also pose challenges and considerations, including:

1. **Regulatory Complexity:** The regulatory landscape for utility tokens is still evolving, and compliance with regional regulations can be a complex issue for token issuers and users.
2. **Scalability:** Some blockchain platforms face scalability challenges as more dApps and users join the network, impacting the performance of utility tokens.

3. **Security:** Smart contracts and dApps involving utility tokens can be vulnerable to vulnerabilities and hacks, emphasizing the importance of security audits.
4. **Interoperability:** The ability of utility tokens to interact and be used across different dApps and ecosystems is a critical aspect that is being actively developed.
5. **Economic Models:** Token economics and governance models are essential for the sustainability and success of utility tokens, requiring careful planning and consideration.

Conclusion

The world of cryptocurrencies extends well beyond Bitcoin, encompassing a diverse landscape of altcoins and utility tokens. Altcoins offer innovative technologies and use cases, while utility tokens provide the means to interact within decentralized applications and ecosystems. Understanding these assets is crucial for those looking to explore the broader cryptocurrency ecosystem and participate in various blockchain-based projects. As you continue your journey into the world of digital assets, keep an eye on emerging altcoins and utility tokens, as they play an increasingly vital role in the ongoing evolution of blockchain technology.

CHAPTER 7:
SECURE YOUR INVESTMENTS

Cryptocurrency Security Best Practices

As you venture into the world of cryptocurrencies, one of your top priorities should be safeguarding your digital assets. Unlike traditional financial systems, cryptocurrencies offer a unique combination of ownership, control, and responsibility. In this chapter, we will explore cryptocurrency security best practices, covering everything from the secure storage of your assets to protecting your investments from various risks.

1. Secure Your Private Keys

Private keys are the keys to your cryptocurrency kingdom. Losing access to your private keys means losing access to your funds. Here are some key practices to ensure the security of your private keys:

- **Use Hardware Wallets:** Consider using hardware wallets for long-term storage. These physical devices store your private keys offline, making them immune to online threats.

- **Back Up Your Keys:** Create multiple backups of your private keys or seed phrases. Store them in different secure locations, such as safety deposit boxes or fireproof safes.

- **Use Secure Passwords:** If you have software wallets, make sure to use strong and unique passwords. Avoid using easily guessable information or reusing passwords.
- **Enable Two-Factor Authentication (2FA):** When available, enable 2FA on your wallets and exchange accounts. 2FA adds an extra layer of security by requiring a one-time code from your mobile device for login.
- **Beware of Phishing:** Be cautious of phishing attempts. Always verify the authenticity of websites and emails. Never enter your private key or seed phrase on suspicious sites.
- **Practice Air-Gapped Transactions:** For added security, conduct air-gapped transactions. This involves signing transactions on a device that is entirely disconnected from the internet.

2. Use Secure Wallets

Choosing the right wallet is a crucial part of cryptocurrency security. Here are the main types of wallets to consider:

- **Hardware Wallets:** These physical devices are considered one of the most secure options. They store your private keys offline and are immune to online threats.
- **Software Wallets:** Software wallets are available as mobile, desktop, or online applications. Use reputable and well-reviewed software wallets, but be cautious of potential vulnerabilities.

- **Paper Wallets:** A paper wallet involves printing your private key or seed phrase on a physical piece of paper. It's highly secure but requires careful handling.
- **Brain Wallets:** Brain wallets rely on memorization. You generate a private key based on a passphrase or a series of words that you commit to memory.
- **Web Wallets:** Be cautious with web wallets, as they are online and can be vulnerable to hacks. Only use web wallets from trusted and reputable sources.

3. Beware of Scams

The cryptocurrency space is not immune to scams and fraudulent schemes. It's essential to be vigilant and skeptical when encountering offers that seem too good to be true. Here are some common scams to watch out for:

- **Ponzi Schemes:** Avoid investment schemes that promise guaranteed high returns. These schemes rely on new investments to pay returns to earlier investors and eventually collapse.
- **Phishing Sites:** Be cautious of websites that mimic legitimate cryptocurrency platforms. Always double-check the website's URL and ensure it's legitimate.
- **Fake ICOs and Tokens:** Conduct thorough research before investing in an Initial Coin Offering (ICO) or a new token. Many scams involve fake projects that raise funds and disappear.
- **Fake Exchanges:** Use well-established and reputable cryptocurrency exchanges. Be cautious of unknown exchanges or platforms that offer questionable services.

- **Impersonation Scams:** Scammers often impersonate influential figures in the crypto space on social media or email. Verify the authenticity of any requests for funds or personal information.

4. Protect Your Identity

Your identity can be a target for fraud or theft, so it's crucial to protect your personal information:

- **Use Pseudonyms:** When creating accounts on exchanges or forums, consider using pseudonyms instead of your real name.
- **Secure Your Personal Information:** Keep personal information, such as your address and phone number, private.
- **Use Secure Email:** Use secure and unique email addresses for cryptocurrency-related accounts. Enable two-factor authentication on your email account.
- **Be Wary of KYC Requests:** Be cautious when sharing your personal information as part of Know Your Customer (KYC) requirements. Only provide it to reputable and regulated platforms.

5. Stay Informed

Staying informed about the latest security threats and best practices is crucial in the ever-evolving world of cryptocurrencies. Here are some ways to stay informed:

- **Follow Reputable News Sources:** Follow cryptocurrency news from reputable sources to keep up with the latest developments, security threats, and regulations.

- **Join Forums and Communities:** Join cryptocurrency forums and communities to engage with experienced users and learn from their insights.
- **Read Whitepapers:** When considering an investment in a new cryptocurrency, read its whitepaper and understand the project's goals, technology, and team.
- **Learn from Security Experts:** Consider learning from security experts or taking online courses in cryptocurrency security.
- **Stay Updated on Regulations:** Be aware of cryptocurrency regulations in your region and how they may impact your investments and activities.

6. Diversify Your Holdings

Diversification is a fundamental risk management strategy. Rather than putting all your funds into a single cryptocurrency, consider spreading your investments across multiple assets. Diversification helps reduce the impact of a single asset's poor performance on your overall portfolio.

7. Set Realistic Goals

It's crucial to set realistic investment goals and manage your expectations. Understand that the cryptocurrency market is highly volatile, and prices can fluctuate significantly in a short period. Don't invest more than you can afford to lose, and avoid making impulsive decisions based on emotions.

Protecting Your Investments

Investing in cryptocurrencies carries its own set of risks, but there are steps you can take to protect your investments and minimize potential losses:

1. Use Stop-Loss Orders

A stop-loss order is a valuable risk management tool. It allows you to set a specific price at which your cryptocurrency holdings will be automatically sold if the market moves against you. This can help limit potential losses and prevent emotional decision-making.

2. Avoid FOMO (Fear of Missing Out)

FOMO is the fear of missing out on potential gains, and it can lead to impulsive decisions. Avoid buying an asset solely because it's rapidly rising in price. Instead, conduct thorough research and make informed investment decisions.

3. Regularly Review Your Portfolio

Regularly review your cryptocurrency portfolio to ensure that it aligns with your investment goals and risk tolerance. Consider rebalancing your holdings if certain assets become overweighted.

4. Set Clear Entry and Exit Strategies

Establish clear entry and exit strategies for your investments. Determine your target price at which you plan to sell or take profits. Having a plan in place can help you avoid making hasty decisions.

5. Keep Emotions in Check

Emotional decisions can lead to losses in the cryptocurrency market. Avoid panic selling during market downturns and don't chase after rapidly rising assets out of fear of missing out. Stick to your investment plan.

6. Use Dollar-Cost Averaging (DCA)

Dollar-cost averaging involves investing a fixed amount of money at regular intervals, regardless of the cryptocurrency's price. This strategy helps mitigate the impact of market volatility and reduces the risk of making large, poorly timed investments.

7. Be Patient and Informed

Cryptocurrency markets can be highly volatile, and prices can fluctuate rapidly. Patience is essential in the crypto space. Make informed decisions based on thorough research and a long-term perspective.

8. Consider Long-Term Holding

Rather than constantly trading or speculating on short-term price movements, consider a long-term holding strategy. Some investors prefer to buy and hold assets with strong fundamentals for an extended period.

9. Use Secure and Reputable Exchanges

Choose reputable and well-established cryptocurrency exchanges for your trading activities. Look for exchanges that prioritize security and regulatory compliance.

10. Stay Informed About Market Trends

Stay informed about market trends and developments in the cryptocurrency space. Market sentiment and news can significantly impact prices, so keeping up with the latest information is essential.

11. Prepare for Tax Obligations

Cryptocurrency transactions can have tax implications, depending on your jurisdiction. Be prepared to meet your tax obligations and keep accurate records of your crypto transactions.

Conclusion

Securing your investments and minimizing risks in the cryptocurrency space require a combination of technical and strategic knowledge. By following cryptocurrency security best practices and implementing sound investment strategies, you can safeguard your assets and make informed decisions in this dynamic and evolving market. Remember that, as with any form of investment, there are no guarantees, and a cautious and well-informed approach is your best ally in the world of cryptocurrencies.

CHAPTER 8: CRYPTOCURRENCY TRADING

Strategies for Success

Cryptocurrency trading is a dynamic and exciting endeavor that can offer opportunities for profit, but it's important to approach it with a well-thought-out strategy. In this chapter, we'll explore various strategies to help you succeed in the world of cryptocurrency trading.

1. Fundamental Analysis

Fundamental analysis involves evaluating a cryptocurrency's intrinsic value by examining its underlying factors. This approach is common in traditional financial markets and can be applied to cryptocurrencies. Key factors to consider include:

- **Technology and Development:** Assess the technology behind the cryptocurrency, its use cases, and its development team. Are there ongoing updates and improvements?
- **Community and Adoption:** The strength of the cryptocurrency's community and its adoption rate can impact its long-term value.

- **Market Demand:** Consider the demand for the cryptocurrency. Is it used in real-world applications, and is there a genuine need for it?
- **Regulatory Environment:** Regulatory developments can have a significant impact on a cryptocurrency's value. Stay informed about regulations in your region.

2. Technical Analysis

Technical analysis involves studying price charts and using indicators to make trading decisions. Some common technical analysis tools and strategies include:

- **Candlestick Patterns:** These patterns help traders identify potential price reversals or continuations.
- **Moving Averages:** Moving averages, such as the simple moving average (SMA) and the exponential moving average (EMA), help identify trends and potential entry or exit points.
- **Relative Strength Index (RSI):** RSI measures the speed and change of price movements and can indicate overbought or oversold conditions.
- **Support and Resistance:** Identify key support and resistance levels to make informed decisions about entry and exit points.
- **Fibonacci Retracement:** This tool helps traders identify potential levels of support or resistance based on the Fibonacci sequence.
- **Bollinger Bands:** These bands can help identify volatility and potential price reversals.

3. Trading Strategies

There are several trading strategies you can consider, depending on your risk tolerance and investment goals:

- **Day Trading:** Day traders aim to profit from short-term price movements. They buy low and sell high within the same day, often making multiple trades.
- **Swing Trading:** Swing traders aim to capture price swings over a period of days or weeks. They may hold positions for longer than day traders but not as long as long-term investors.
- **Scalping:** Scalpers make quick, small trades to capture tiny price movements. This strategy requires a high level of focus and quick execution.
- **Hodling (Holding):** Long-term investors, often referred to as "Hodlers," buy and hold cryptocurrencies for an extended period, typically ignoring short-term price fluctuations.
- **Arbitrage:** Arbitrage involves exploiting price differences for the same cryptocurrency on different exchanges. Traders buy low on one exchange and sell high on another, profiting from the price differential.
- **Margin Trading:** Margin trading allows traders to borrow funds to increase their position size. This strategy amplifies both gains and losses and carries higher risk.
- **Algorithmic Trading:** Some traders use algorithms and automated trading bots to execute trades based on predefined criteria.

4. Risk Management

Risk management is crucial in cryptocurrency trading. Implement the following risk management practices:

- **Position Sizing:** Determine how much of your capital you're willing to risk on each trade. A common rule is to risk no more than 1-2% of your capital on a single trade.
- **Stop-Loss Orders:** Set stop-loss orders to limit potential losses. These orders automatically sell your position if the price reaches a specified level.
- **Take-Profit Orders:** Take-profit orders specify the price at which you want to secure profits. They help you avoid greed-driven decisions.
- **Diversification:** Diversify your portfolio to spread risk across different assets. Avoid putting all your capital into a single cryptocurrency.
- **Risk-Reward Ratio:** Before entering a trade, calculate the potential risk-reward ratio. Ensure that the potential reward justifies the risk you're taking.
- **Emotion Control:** Emotions can lead to impulsive decisions. Stick to your trading plan, and don't let fear or greed dictate your actions.

5. Continuous Learning

The cryptocurrency market is ever-evolving, and it's essential to stay informed and continuously learn. Here are some ways to expand your knowledge:

- **Read Books and Articles:** Explore books and articles on cryptocurrency trading and market analysis.

- **Take Online Courses:** Numerous online courses offer in-depth knowledge and strategies for cryptocurrency trading.
- **Follow Experienced Traders:** Follow experienced traders on social media and learn from their insights and strategies.
- **Practice in a Demo Account:** Some exchanges and platforms offer demo accounts where you can practice trading without risking real money.
- **Attend Conferences and Webinars:** Cryptocurrency conferences and webinars can provide valuable insights and networking opportunities.

Avoiding Common Pitfalls

While developing a trading strategy is important, avoiding common pitfalls is equally crucial. Here are some pitfalls to watch out for:

1. Overtrading

Overtrading occurs when you make too many trades, often fueled by impulsive decisions. This can lead to excessive transaction fees and losses. To avoid overtrading:

- Stick to your trading plan.
- Set clear criteria for entering and exiting trades.
- Avoid making emotional decisions based on FOMO (fear of missing out) or fear of loss.

2. Neglecting Security

Neglecting security can lead to the loss of your cryptocurrency assets. Be mindful of the following security practices:

- Use secure wallets and exchanges.
- Enable two-factor authentication (2FA) on all your accounts.
- Store private keys and seed phrases securely.

3. Ignoring Fundamental Analysis

While technical analysis is valuable, ignoring fundamental analysis can lead to investments in weak or fraudulent projects. Take time to understand the fundamentals of the cryptocurrencies you invest in.

4. Chasing Hype and Fads

Chasing hype and fads often results in buying assets at their peak and suffering losses when the market cools off. Avoid making investment decisions solely based on social media hype and rumors.

5. Neglecting Risk Management

Neglecting risk management can result in significant losses. Implement sound risk management practices, including position sizing, stop-loss orders, and diversification.

6. Lack of Patience

Impatience can lead to panic selling during market downturns. Develop the patience to ride out market fluctuations and stick to your long-term strategy.

7. Falling for Scams

The cryptocurrency space is not free of scams. Be wary of Ponzi schemes, fraudulent ICOs, and phishing attempts. Always conduct due diligence before investing.

8. Emotional Trading

Emotions like greed and fear can drive impulsive decisions. Stick to your trading plan and avoid making emotional trades. Remember that cryptocurrency markets can be highly volatile.

9. Ignoring Taxes

Ignoring tax obligations can lead to legal issues. Be prepared to report and pay taxes on cryptocurrency gains in your jurisdiction.

10. Failing to Adapt

The cryptocurrency market is continuously evolving. Failing to adapt to new trends, technologies, and regulations can result in missed opportunities and losses.

Conclusion

Cryptocurrency trading offers both opportunities and risks. Success in the market requires a combination of strategies, continuous learning, and the discipline to avoid common pitfalls. Whether you're a day trader, a long-term investor, or somewhere in between, the key to success is informed decision-making, prudent risk management, and a keen eye on market dynamics. Keep in mind that trading cryptocurrencies involves a level of risk, and it's essential to only invest what you can afford to lose while striving for success in this exciting and evolving market.

CHAPTER 9:
INITIAL COIN OFFERINGS (ICOS) AND TOKEN SALES

What Are ICOs?

In the world of cryptocurrencies, Initial Coin Offerings (ICOs) and token sales have gained prominence as a means for blockchain projects to raise capital and distribute their tokens to a wider audience. An ICO is a fundraising method that involves the issuance of new cryptocurrency tokens or coins to investors and early supporters of a project in exchange for established cryptocurrencies like Bitcoin (BTC) or Ethereum (ETH). In this chapter, we will explore the concept of ICOs and the key aspects associated with them.

The Birth of ICOs

ICOs gained widespread attention and popularity in the cryptocurrency space around 2017, but their history can be traced back to earlier initiatives. Mastercoin (now known as Omni) conducted the first recorded ICO in 2013, aiming to create a layer on top of the Bitcoin blockchain for additional features. This event set the stage for future token sales.

Ethereum's ICO in 2014 was a significant turning point. Ethereum, led by Vitalik Buterin, raised over $18 million, enabling the development of the Ethereum blockchain. Ethereum's success inspired numerous other projects to consider ICOs as a viable method for fundraising.

How ICOs Work

ICOs are typically launched by blockchain projects, startups, or development teams seeking capital to fund their projects and platforms. Here's a step-by-step overview of how ICOs work:

1. Project Idea and Whitepaper: A project team conceives an idea for a blockchain-based platform, application, or service. They outline their vision and technical details in a whitepaper, which serves as a comprehensive document explaining the project's goals, technology, token structure, and fundraising details.

2. Token Creation: The project team creates a new cryptocurrency token that will be distributed during the ICO. These tokens are often built on existing blockchain platforms like Ethereum (ERC-20 tokens), Binance Smart Chain (BEP-20 tokens), or others.

3. Marketing and Hype: Before the ICO launch, project teams engage in marketing and promotion to generate interest and attract potential investors. This may involve social media campaigns, community building, and partnerships.

4. ICO Launch: The ICO commences on a specified date and typically lasts for a specific period, during which investors can contribute funds in exchange for the newly created tokens.

5. Token Distribution: After the ICO concludes, the project team distributes the purchased tokens to investors. These tokens can be held in cryptocurrency wallets or traded on cryptocurrency exchanges.

6. Development and Roadmap: With the funds raised from the ICO, the project team proceeds with the development of their platform, application, or service as outlined in their whitepaper. They aim to fulfill the promises made to investors.

7. Token Utility: The tokens issued during the ICO may have various utilities within the project's ecosystem. These utilities can include access to the platform, voting rights, or the ability to pay for services.

Why ICOs Are Attractive

ICOs have garnered interest for several reasons:

1. Access to Early-Stage Projects: ICOs allow investors to access early-stage projects and tokens that may have significant potential for growth.

2. Liquidity: Tokens acquired during an ICO can often be traded on cryptocurrency exchanges, providing liquidity to investors.

3. Diversification: Investors can diversify their cryptocurrency portfolio by participating in different ICOs across various projects.

4. Investment Opportunities: ICOs offer opportunities to invest in projects and technologies that align with an investor's interests and beliefs.

Evaluating ICO Investments

Investing in ICOs can be rewarding but also comes with substantial risks. To make informed investment decisions, it's essential to evaluate ICOs carefully. Here are key factors to consider:

1. Whitepaper Analysis:

- Review the project's whitepaper to understand its goals, technology, and vision. Assess whether the project addresses a real problem and whether its solutions are feasible.

2. Team and Advisors:

- Investigate the project's development team and advisory board. Assess their experience, qualifications, and track record in the blockchain and cryptocurrency industry.

3. Use Case and Utility:

- Understand the use case of the project's token. Does the token have a clear utility within the project's ecosystem, or is it primarily speculative?

4. Roadmap and Milestones:

- Evaluate the project's roadmap and the milestones it aims to achieve. Is there a clear plan for development, and are there measurable goals?

5. Community and Support:

- Examine the size and engagement of the project's community. A strong and supportive community can contribute to a project's success.

6. Security and Audits:

- Check whether the project has undergone security audits to identify and mitigate vulnerabilities. Security is crucial, especially in the context of smart contracts.

7. Token Economics:

- Analyze the token distribution and economics. Are there vesting periods for team members and advisors to ensure their long-term commitment to the project?

8. Regulatory Compliance:

- Be aware of the project's approach to regulatory compliance. Some ICOs may restrict participation from certain regions to comply with local laws.

9. Partnerships and Alliances:

- Look for partnerships and alliances with reputable organizations. These partnerships can provide credibility and support for the project.

10. Token Sale Terms:

- Understand the terms of the ICO, including the fundraising goal, hard cap, soft cap, and token price. Ensure that the terms align with your investment goals and risk tolerance.

11. Market Sentiment:

- Monitor the sentiment surrounding the project and its ICO in the cryptocurrency community. A positive reputation can contribute to the project's success.

12. Due Diligence:

- Conduct thorough due diligence before participating in any ICO. This includes researching the project, team, and technology, as well as understanding the risks involved.

Risks Associated with ICOs

ICOs can be highly speculative and come with various risks, including:

- **Regulatory Uncertainty:** The regulatory landscape for ICOs is evolving, and projects may face legal challenges or changes in regulations.
- **Lack of Transparency:** Some ICOs may lack transparency in their operations and financials, making it challenging to assess their legitimacy.
- **Market Volatility:** The cryptocurrency market is known for its volatility, which can affect the value of ICO tokens.
- **Scams and Fraud:** The lack of regulation can lead to fraudulent ICOs or projects with no intention of delivering on their promises.
- **Project Failure:** Not all projects succeed, and some ICOs may result in the loss of invested funds if the project fails to materialize.
- **Lack of Investor Protections:** ICO investors may have limited legal protections in case of disputes or issues with the project.

Conclusion

ICOs have played a significant role in the growth of the cryptocurrency industry by providing a means for blockchain projects to raise capital and engage with a global audience. However, investing in ICOs carries risks, and thorough research and due diligence are crucial when evaluating potential investments. The cryptocurrency market continues to evolve, and ICOs remain a dynamic aspect of this space. As an investor, staying informed and cautious is paramount when considering ICO participation, helping you make informed decisions and manage risks effectively.

CHAPTER 10:
THE FUTURE OF CRYPTO

Emerging Trends and Innovations

The cryptocurrency landscape is continually evolving, with new trends and innovations shaping the industry's future. In this chapter, we'll explore the exciting developments that are driving the future of crypto.

1. Decentralized Finance (DeFi)

DeFi, short for Decentralized Finance, is one of the most revolutionary trends in the cryptocurrency industry. DeFi applications aim to recreate traditional financial services such as lending, borrowing, trading, and asset management using blockchain technology. Key components of DeFi include:

- **Decentralized Exchanges (DEXs):** These platforms allow users to trade cryptocurrencies without the need for a centralized intermediary. Notable DEXs include Uniswap, SushiSwap, and PancakeSwap.
- **Lending and Borrowing Protocols:** DeFi offers lending and borrowing platforms where users can lend their cryptocurrencies to earn interest or borrow

assets by providing collateral. Examples include Compound and Aave.

- **Yield Farming:** Yield farming involves users providing liquidity to DeFi platforms in exchange for rewards or interest. It's a way to generate returns on cryptocurrency holdings.
- **Synthetic Assets:** Some DeFi projects enable the creation of synthetic assets that track the value of real-world assets, such as stocks, commodities, or fiat currencies.
- **Automated Market Makers (AMMs):** AMMs facilitate liquidity provision and asset swapping, simplifying trading on DEXs.

DeFi has grown significantly, with billions of dollars locked in DeFi protocols. However, it also faces challenges related to security, regulation, and scalability. As the DeFi ecosystem matures, it's likely to become a more integral part of the broader financial landscape.

2. Non-Fungible Tokens (NFTs)

Non-Fungible Tokens (NFTs) are unique digital assets that represent ownership of a specific item, piece of art, collectible, or digital content. NFTs are indivisible and cannot be exchanged on a one-to-one basis like cryptocurrencies. Key features of NFTs include:

- **Ownership and Provenance:** NFTs provide proof of ownership and the history of a digital item. This has applications in art, music, gaming, and even real estate.

- **Digital Collectibles:** NFTs have become popular for digital collectibles and gaming items. They allow players to truly own in-game assets.
- **Art and Creativity:** NFTs have created a new market for digital artists and creators, offering a way to monetize their work.
- **Ownership of Virtual Land:** Some virtual worlds and games sell virtual land as NFTs, allowing users to own and develop digital real estate.

NFTs have made headlines with high-value sales of digital art and collectibles. They have also raised discussions about copyright, intellectual property, and the ownership of digital goods. The NFT space is likely to continue evolving with new use cases and innovations.

3. Central Bank Digital Currencies (CBDCs)

Central Bank Digital Currencies, or **CBDCs**, are digital versions of a country's national currency issued and regulated by the central bank. Unlike cryptocurrencies, CBDCs are fully controlled by governments and are considered legal tender. Key aspects of CBDCs include:

- **Digital Cash:** CBDCs provide a digital form of cash, allowing citizens to transact using a digital wallet issued by the central bank.
- **Financial Inclusion:** CBDCs have the potential to improve financial inclusion by providing access to banking services for unbanked or underbanked populations.
- **Regulatory Compliance:** CBDCs are issued and regulated by central banks, ensuring they comply with local regulations and monetary policies.

- **Cross-Border Transactions:** CBDCs can simplify and expedite cross-border transactions, reducing costs and delays.

Numerous countries, including China, Sweden, and the United States, are exploring the development of CBDCs. These digital currencies have the potential to reshape the financial landscape, providing a digital alternative to physical cash.

4. Layer 2 Scaling Solutions

The issue of scalability has been a long-standing challenge for blockchain networks, particularly for Ethereum. **Layer 2 scaling solutions** aim to address this problem by building additional layers on top of existing blockchains. Key solutions include:

- **Sidechains:** Sidechains are independent blockchains connected to the main blockchain. They can process transactions more quickly and with lower fees.
- **Plasma:** Plasma is a framework for creating scalable and secure smart contracts on the Ethereum blockchain. It allows multiple child chains to interact with the main chain.
- **State Channels:** State channels enable off-chain transactions, allowing users to conduct a series of transactions without involving the main blockchain for every step.
- **Rollups:** Rollup solutions, like Optimistic Rollups and ZK-Rollups, aggregate multiple transactions into a single one and then submit them to the main blockchain, reducing congestion and gas fees.

Layer 2 scaling solutions aim to enhance the scalability of blockchain networks while maintaining the security and decentralization of the underlying chain. These solutions are expected to play a significant role in the future of blockchain technology.

5. Blockchain Interoperability

Blockchain interoperability refers to the ability of different blockchain networks to communicate and share data. It addresses the fragmentation and lack of communication between various blockchain platforms. Key components of blockchain interoperability include:

- **Cross-Chain Platforms:** Projects like Polkadot and Cosmos aim to create cross-chain ecosystems that allow different blockchains to interoperate.
- **Bridge Protocols:** Bridge protocols enable the transfer of assets and data between blockchains. These bridges facilitate cross-chain transactions and interactions.
- **Interoperability Standards:** The development of interoperability standards can help ensure that different blockchains can communicate seamlessly.

Blockchain interoperability is essential for the growth of the blockchain ecosystem, as it allows different networks to leverage each other's strengths and capabilities.

Regulatory Landscape

The regulatory environment for cryptocurrencies and blockchain technology is rapidly evolving as governments and regulatory bodies grapple with how to address this innovative space. It's important to understand the current and future regulatory landscape to navigate the world of crypto effectively.

1. Regulatory Challenges

Cryptocurrency regulations vary significantly from one country to another, creating a complex and often uncertain landscape. Some of the key regulatory challenges include:

- **Classification:** Governments struggle to classify cryptocurrencies. Are they securities, commodities, or currencies?
- **Taxation:** Determining how to tax cryptocurrency transactions and gains is a complex issue.
- **Consumer Protection:** Protecting consumers from fraud, scams, and hacks is a priority for regulators.
- **AML and KYC:** Implementing anti-money laundering (AML) and know your customer (KYC) regulations is crucial to prevent illegal activities.
- **Cross-Border Transactions:** The global nature of cryptocurrencies makes cross-border transactions and regulatory coordination challenging.
- **Innovation vs. Regulation:** Striking a balance between fostering blockchain innovation and protecting investors is an ongoing challenge.

2. Evolving Regulations

Governments worldwide are actively working on cryptocurrency regulations, but these efforts are at different stages of development:

- **United States:** The U.S. is working to establish a comprehensive regulatory framework for cryptocurrencies. Several regulatory agencies, including the

SEC and CFTC, have jurisdiction over different aspects of the industry.

- **European Union:** The EU is exploring regulation for cryptocurrencies to establish a unified approach across member states. The EU's Markets in Crypto-Assets (MiCA) proposal aims to create a regulatory framework.
- **China:** China has implemented strict regulations on cryptocurrencies, including bans on initial coin offerings (ICOs) and cryptocurrency exchanges. However, they are developing their digital currency, the digital yuan.
- **India:** India has had a tumultuous relationship with cryptocurrencies. The government has proposed bans on cryptocurrency trading, but the legal status remains uncertain.
- **Other Countries:** Many countries are considering regulations or have implemented them to varying degrees. Some are embracing cryptocurrencies and blockchain technology, while others are taking a more cautious approach.

3. Impact on the Industry

Regulations have a significant impact on the cryptocurrency industry, affecting exchanges, projects, and individual investors:

- **Exchanges:** Cryptocurrency exchanges often need to comply with AML and KYC regulations. Some jurisdictions require licensing, while others prohibit certain activities.

- **Projects:** Blockchain projects must consider legal and regulatory compliance, particularly in their fund-raising efforts. ICOs and token sales are subject to securities laws in many jurisdictions.
- **Investors:** Investors need to be aware of tax obligations and reporting requirements in their respective jurisdictions.

4. The Path Forward

The regulatory landscape for cryptocurrencies is still unfolding, and it's likely to continue evolving over the coming years. As the industry matures, it's important for governments and regulatory bodies to strike a balance between ensuring investor protection, fostering innovation, and allowing the blockchain and crypto space to thrive.

The future of crypto regulation may involve:

- **Global Coordination:** Collaboration among countries to create international standards and promote cross-border regulatory consistency.
- **Clarity:** Clear and comprehensive regulations that provide legal certainty for individuals and businesses operating in the cryptocurrency space.
- **Innovation-Friendly Policies:** Regulatory environments that support blockchain technology and the growth of the industry.
- **Educational Initiatives:** Public awareness and educational efforts to help individuals understand the risks and benefits of cryptocurrencies.
- **Adaptability:** Regulations that can adapt to the rapidly changing technological landscape and market dynamics.

Conclusion

Emerging trends and innovations like DeFi, NFTs, CBDCs, Layer 2 scaling solutions, and blockchain interoperability are reshaping the industry. At the same time, the regulatory landscape is maturing and evolving, with governments and regulators taking various approaches to address the challenges and opportunities presented by cryptocurrencies and blockchain technology.

To navigate this future successfully, participants in the crypto space, whether investors, developers, or entrepreneurs, need to stay informed, adapt to changing regulations, and harness the innovative potential of blockchain technology. As the industry continues to mature, it will be fascinating to witness how these dynamics play out and how they shape the future of crypto on a global scale.

CHAPTER 11: PRACTICAL USE CASES

Cryptocurrency in Everyday Life

Cryptocurrencies, once a niche concept, have become increasingly integrated into everyday life. Their use cases extend beyond investment and speculation, with cryptocurrencies offering practical solutions for a range of daily activities. In this chapter, we will explore how cryptocurrencies have found their place in the world of commerce, finance, and beyond.

1. Online Payments

One of the most evident use cases for cryptocurrencies in everyday life is online payments. Cryptocurrencies provide a fast, secure, and borderless way to make online transactions. Some key aspects of online payments with cryptocurrencies include:

- **Global Accessibility:** Cryptocurrencies can be used worldwide, eliminating the need for currency conversion.
- **Reduced Transaction Costs:** Traditional payment methods, such as credit cards and international bank

transfers, often involve high fees. Cryptocurrency transactions can be cost-effective, especially for cross-border payments.

- **Privacy:** Cryptocurrencies can offer a degree of privacy, as transaction details can be pseudonymous. However, it's essential to remember that not all cryptocurrencies provide complete anonymity.
- **Instant Transactions:** Many cryptocurrencies allow for near-instant transactions, making them suitable for e-commerce and online services.
- **Micropayments:** Cryptocurrencies enable the facilitation of micropayments, making it feasible to pay small amounts for digital content, services, or goods.
- **User Control:** Cryptocurrency users have control over their funds and transactions, reducing the reliance on intermediaries like banks.

Popular cryptocurrencies like Bitcoin and Ethereum are accepted by an increasing number of online retailers and service providers, making it easier for people to use digital assets for everyday purchases.

2. Remittances

Cryptocurrencies have the potential to revolutionize the remittance industry. Traditional remittance services are often slow and expensive, especially for cross-border transfers. Cryptocurrencies address these challenges with several advantages:

- **Speed:** Cryptocurrency transactions can be processed quickly, providing faster remittance services.

- **Lower Costs:** Cryptocurrencies typically involve lower fees, reducing the cost of sending money to family and friends abroad.
- **Accessibility:** Cryptocurrencies can be sent and received by anyone with internet access and a cryptocurrency wallet, making it easier for unbanked or underbanked individuals to receive funds.
- **Borderless:** Cryptocurrencies are not constrained by national borders, simplifying cross-border remittances.

Several blockchain projects and startups are working on solutions for cross-border remittances, leveraging cryptocurrencies to provide more efficient and affordable alternatives to traditional services.

3. Investment and Savings

Cryptocurrencies have become an investment vehicle for individuals looking to diversify their portfolios or take advantage of the potential for significant returns. Key aspects of cryptocurrency investments and savings include:

- **Store of Value:** Some view cryptocurrencies like Bitcoin as a store of value similar to gold, with the potential to retain or increase in value over time.
- **Speculation:** Cryptocurrency markets can be highly speculative, with traders looking to profit from price fluctuations.
- **Hedging:** Investors may use cryptocurrencies as a hedge against economic instability, currency devaluation, or political turmoil in their home countries.

- **Savings Accounts:** Some platforms offer cryptocurrency savings accounts, allowing users to earn interest on their crypto holdings.
- **Diversification:** Cryptocurrencies can provide a means of diversifying an investment portfolio, spreading risk across different asset classes.

It's important to approach cryptocurrency investments with caution and conduct thorough research, as the market can be highly volatile.

4. Gaming and Virtual Assets

The gaming industry has seen a significant integration of cryptocurrencies and blockchain technology. Cryptocurrencies have found applications in gaming, especially in the form of non-fungible tokens (NFTs) and virtual assets. Key uses in the gaming industry include:

- **Ownership of In-Game Items:** NFTs allow gamers to own in-game assets and characters as unique, tradable tokens.
- **Virtual Economies:** Cryptocurrencies and tokens are used within virtual game economies, enabling in-game purchases, trading, and incentives.
- **Cross-Game Compatibility:** Some blockchain platforms aim to create interoperability between different games, allowing assets to move seamlessly from one game to another.
- **Blockchain-Based Games:** Entire games are built on blockchain technology, offering decentralized and provably fair gameplay.

The integration of cryptocurrencies in the gaming industry is creating new possibilities for gamers, game developers, and content creators.

5. Donations and Crowdfunding

Cryptocurrencies have found applications in the realms of charity, donations, and crowdfunding. They offer several advantages for individuals and organizations looking to raise funds:

- **Transparency:** Blockchain technology provides transparency in the flow of funds, allowing donors to track the use of their contributions.
- **Lower Transaction Costs:** Cryptocurrencies can reduce the fees associated with transferring donations, ensuring that a larger portion of funds reaches the intended recipients.
- **Global Donations:** Cryptocurrencies facilitate global donations, making it easier for individuals to contribute to causes and organizations worldwide.
- **Smart Contracts:** Smart contracts can automate the distribution of funds based on predefined criteria, ensuring that donations are used for their intended purpose.

Cryptocurrencies have been used for disaster relief, charitable causes, and crowdfunding campaigns, offering a new way to support various initiatives.

Real-World Applications of Blockchain

Beyond cryptocurrencies, blockchain technology itself has found practical applications in various industries. Blockchain's core features, including transparency, immutability, and security, make it suitable for a range of real-world use cases. Let's explore some of the industries and applications where blockchain technology is making a significant impact.

1. Supply Chain Management

Blockchain technology is transforming supply chain management by enhancing transparency, traceability, and efficiency. Key aspects of blockchain in supply chain management include:

- **Provenance Tracking:** Blockchain can track the origin and journey of products from manufacturer to end consumer, reducing the risk of counterfeiting and ensuring quality.
- **Efficient Record-Keeping:** Blockchain simplifies record-keeping and documentation processes, reducing errors and disputes.
- **Quality Assurance:** Blockchain provides immutable records that can verify the quality and authenticity of products, particularly in industries like food, pharmaceuticals, and luxury goods.
- **Real-Time Visibility:** Blockchain enables real-time monitoring of the supply chain, allowing stakeholders to identify and address issues promptly.

Prominent companies and organizations are implementing blockchain solutions to optimize their supply chain processes and enhance trust in their products.

2. Healthcare

Blockchain technology is revolutionizing the healthcare industry by improving data security, interoperability, and patient care. Key uses of blockchain in healthcare include:

- **Electronic Health Records (EHRs):** Blockchain can securely store and manage electronic health records, giving patients more control over their data.
- **Data Sharing:** Patients can share their medical data with healthcare providers or researchers securely, promoting collaborative care and medical research.
- **Drug Traceability:** Blockchain can trace the origins and distribution of pharmaceuticals to ensure authenticity and prevent counterfeit drugs.
- **Clinical Trials:** Blockchain can enhance the transparency and integrity of clinical trial data, potentially expediting drug development.

Blockchain-based healthcare solutions aim to increase data security, patient privacy, and the efficiency of healthcare services.

3. Voting and Elections

Blockchain technology has the potential to address challenges related to electoral integrity and secure voting systems. Key benefits of blockchain in voting systems include:

- **Immutable Records:** Blockchain ensures that once a vote is recorded, it cannot be altered or deleted, providing an accurate and transparent voting history.
- **Remote Voting:** Blockchain can enable secure remote voting, allowing eligible voters to participate in elections from anywhere.
- **Enhanced Transparency:** The transparent and publicly accessible nature of blockchain can improve trust in the electoral process.

- **Reduced Fraud:** Blockchain technology can help prevent voter fraud and ensure the integrity of elections.

While blockchain-based voting systems are still in the experimental phase in many regions, they hold the potential to transform electoral processes in the future.

4. Intellectual Property

Blockchain technology can be used to protect intellectual property rights, particularly in the fields of art, music, and content creation. Key aspects of blockchain in intellectual property include:

- **Copyright Management:** Artists and creators can register their work on a blockchain to prove ownership and protect against copyright infringement.
- **Royalty Payments:** Smart contracts can automate royalty payments to content creators, ensuring they receive fair compensation for their work.
- **Authentication:** Blockchain can verify the authenticity of digital art and collectibles, preventing counterfeiting.
- **Marketplaces:** Blockchain-based marketplaces allow artists to sell their work directly to consumers, eliminating intermediaries.

Blockchain is helping artists and creators gain more control over their intellectual property and revenue streams.

5. Real Estate

Blockchain technology is being applied to streamline real estate transactions and improve transparency in property management. Key uses in real estate include:

- **Property Ownership:** Blockchain can securely record property ownership, reducing the risk of fraud and simplifying title transfers.
- **Smart Contracts:** Smart contracts can automate property transactions, ensuring that all parties meet their obligations.
- **Fractional Ownership:** Blockchain enables fractional ownership, making it easier for individuals to invest in real estate.
- **Property Records:** Immutable blockchain records can store and retrieve property-related data, reducing administrative errors.

Blockchain's impact on the real estate industry is expected to grow as more organizations adopt blockchain solutions.

6. Energy and Sustainability

Blockchain technology is being harnessed to enhance the management of energy resources, increase sustainability, and reduce carbon emissions. Key applications in the energy sector include:

- **Peer-to-Peer Energy Trading:** Blockchain can facilitate peer-to-peer energy trading, allowing individuals and businesses to buy and sell excess energy directly.
- **Carbon Credits:** Blockchain can track and verify carbon credits, ensuring the legitimacy of carbon offset programs.
- **Grid Management:** Blockchain can improve the efficiency of energy grid management by enabling real-time data sharing and automation.

- **Supply Chain Traceability:** Blockchain can track the origins of renewable energy sources, such as solar or wind power.

Blockchain's role in the energy sector supports the transition toward cleaner and more sustainable energy sources.

Conclusion

The practical use cases of cryptocurrencies and blockchain technology have expanded far beyond their original intentions. Cryptocurrencies have found their place in everyday life, serving as a means of online payment, remittance, investment, and more. Meanwhile, blockchain technology is transforming various industries by enhancing transparency, security, and efficiency. From supply chain management to healthcare, voting systems, intellectual property, real estate, and energy, blockchain is reshaping traditional processes and enabling new possibilities.

As the adoption of cryptocurrencies and blockchain technology continues to grow, it's clear that they are here to stay and will continue to shape the future of commerce, finance, and various other sectors. Understanding these practical use cases is crucial for individuals, businesses, and industries looking to leverage the potential of this innovative technology.

CONCLUSION: EMBRACING THE FUTURE OF MONEY

In the pages of "Crypto Clarity: Demystifying Bitcoin and Blockchain for Beginners," we've embarked on a fascinating journey through the world of cryptocurrencies and blockchain technology. From the humble beginnings of Bitcoin to the vast landscape of blockchain applications, we've covered the essential knowledge and tools needed to navigate this revolutionary space. As we conclude this book, it's vital to reflect on the significance of what we've explored and the profound impact cryptocurrencies and blockchain technology are having on our world.

A Paradigm Shift in Finance

The rise of cryptocurrencies marks a paradigm shift in the world of finance and economics. Traditional financial systems have long been characterized by centralized control, intermediaries, and geographic limitations. Cryptocurrencies challenge these conventions by introducing decentralized, borderless, and trustless systems.

At the heart of this transformation is the pioneering cryptocurrency, Bitcoin. Bitcoin represents a radical departure from conventional currency and a new way of thinking about money. It's digital, secure, and entirely peer-to-peer, eliminating the need for banks, payment processors, or governments to mediate financial transactions. The invention of Bitcoin and the underlying blockchain technology introduces a novel concept: digital scarcity. Unlike fiat currencies, which can be printed in unlimited quantities, Bitcoin is limited to 21 million coins, creating a deflationary model.

The impact of Bitcoin extends beyond its use as a store of value and a medium of exchange. It embodies a philosophy of financial sovereignty, empowering individuals to take control of their wealth and engage in borderless commerce. Bitcoin represents a promise of a more inclusive and equitable financial system.

The Expanding Landscape of Blockchain Technology

Blockchain technology, the backbone of cryptocurrencies like Bitcoin, has far-reaching applications that transcend the realm of finance. We've explored how blockchain is revolutionizing industries across the board, from supply chain management and healthcare to voting systems and intellectual property protection.

Blockchain's key features, such as transparency, immutability, and decentralization, make it a powerful tool for addressing inefficiencies and fostering trust in various sectors. It has the potential to eliminate fraudulent practices, reduce costs, and enhance security. The examples we've discussed in this book are just the tip of the iceberg. Innovators are continually discovering new applications for blockchain, expanding the possibilities of what can be achieved.

The future of blockchain technology is filled with exciting prospects. As industries continue to embrace blockchain, we can anticipate greater efficiency, more secure data management, and increased transparency in various fields. These advancements will impact our daily lives and the way organizations operate, streamlining processes, and ensuring the integrity of transactions and records.

Navigating the Cryptocurrency Landscape

Understanding the cryptocurrency landscape and how to navigate it is paramount for anyone looking to participate in this groundbreaking era. In this book, we've provided a comprehensive guide for beginners, outlining the essential steps for entering the world of cryptocurrencies. We've covered the basics, including what cryptocurrencies are, how they work, and the different types of wallets. You've learned how to buy your first cryptocurrency and secure your investment through various methods. Additionally, we've emphasized the importance of researching cryptocurrency projects and building a diversified portfolio.

But the journey doesn't end with this book. The cryptocurrency space is dynamic, continuously evolving, and often challenging to predict. As you venture into this world, it's essential to keep a few guiding principles in mind:

1. Education Is Ongoing

Cryptocurrencies and blockchain technology are intricate and evolving fields. Continuously expanding your knowledge and staying informed about the latest developments is essential. The cryptocurrency community is vibrant, with forums, online communities, conferences, and educational resources. Engage with this community, ask questions, and remain curious.

2. Security Is Paramount

Security is of the utmost importance in the cryptocurrency space. Always use strong passwords and enable two-factor authentication (2FA) for your accounts. Back up your wallet securely, be cautious of scams and phishing attempts, and consider using hardware wallets for long-term storage. Stay vigilant and protect your investments.

3. Diversification Matters

Diversifying your cryptocurrency portfolio is a proven strategy for managing risk. Avoid putting all your funds into a single asset. Different cryptocurrencies have unique features and potential for growth. Diversification can help you spread risk and enhance your chances of success.

4. Plan Your Exit Strategy

An exit strategy is essential for making informed investment decisions. Decide when and how you'll sell or convert your cryptocurrencies. Consider your profit goals, risk tolerance, and tax implications. By planning your exit strategy, you'll make more deliberate and thoughtful decisions about your investments.

5. Regulatory Awareness

Cryptocurrency regulations vary by country and are continually evolving. Stay informed about the regulatory landscape in your region and consider the implications for your investments and transactions. Compliance with tax laws is crucial to avoid legal complications.

6. Long-Term Vision

While it's tempting to focus on short-term gains and market fluctuations, keeping a long-term perspective can be rewarding. The cryptocurrency market can be highly volatile, but it has shown resilience and growth over the years. Understand the projects you invest in, assess their long-term potential, and make decisions that align with your goals.

The Future Awaits

As we close this chapter, it's essential to recognize that cryptocurrencies and blockchain technology are only beginning to shape our future. The potential applications and transformative power of this technology are vast, and it will influence how we conduct business, handle data, and manage our financial affairs for years to come.

Cryptocurrencies and blockchain have transcended mere technological innovations; they represent a societal shift towards financial self-sovereignty, decentralized governance, and trust in code. They're creating opportunities for financial inclusion, economic empowerment, and innovation. The possibilities are limitless, and the world is beginning to take notice.

This book has aimed to provide you with the foundation and knowledge to embark on your cryptocurrency journey. It's a world filled with excitement, innovation, and, yes, risks. But it's also a world of potential rewards and the chance to participate in a groundbreaking shift in how we perceive and handle value.

As we part ways, remember that the future is yours to shape. Whether you're interested in investing, building on the blockchain, or simply understanding the technology that's transforming industries, your journey has only just begun. The cryptocurrency landscape is constantly evolving, and you have the tools and knowledge to navigate it with confidence.

So, with a spirit of curiosity and a dash of courage, venture forth into the realm of cryptocurrencies and blockchain. Continue learning, adapt to changes, and be part of the ongoing narrative of this transformative era. The future of money and the possibilities it holds are at your fingertips. The digital frontier beckons.

www.ingramcontent.com/pod-product-compliance
Lightning Source LLC
Chambersburg PA
CBHW072331290526
45794CB00002B/825

* 9 7 9 8 8 6 5 7 7 2 8 1 1 *